48032379

PowerPhonics™

All Sorts of Sports

Learning the OR Sound

Susan Hogenkamp

The Rosen Publishing Group's
PowerKids Press™
New York

There are all sorts of sports.

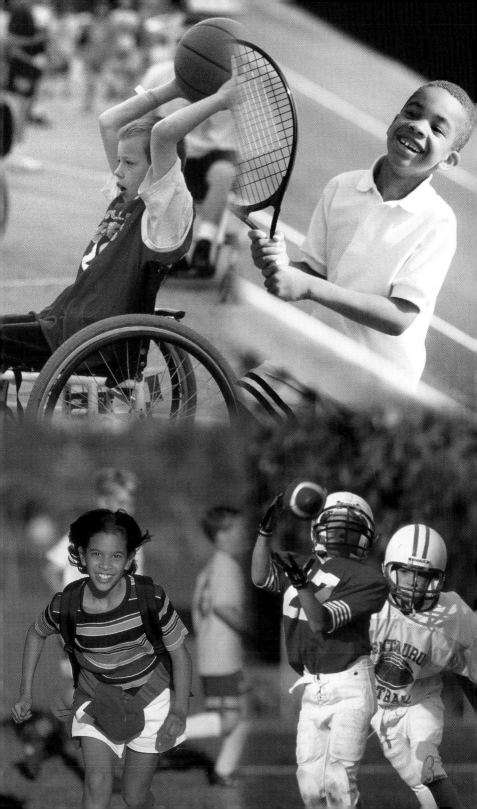

Baseball is a sport.

I score a run for my team.

Soccer is a sport.

I yell for my team to score.

Running is a sport.

I run in shorts.

Shorts

Swimming is a sport.

I wear swim shorts.

Shorts

What sort of sport do you like best?

21

Word List

for

score

shorts

sort

sport

Instructional Guide

Note to Instructors:

One of the essential skills that enable a young child to read is the ability to associate letter-sound symbols and blend these sounds to form words. Phonics instruction can teach children a system that will help them decode unfamiliar words and, in turn, enhance their word-recognition skills. We offer a phonics-based series of books that are easy to read and understand. Each book pairs words and pictures that reinforce specific phonetic sounds in a logical sequence. Topics are based on curriculum goals appropriate for early readers in the areas of science, social studies, and health.

Letters/Sound: or – Write the word *or* and have the child read it. Pronounce the following pairs of words, having the child tell in which one they hear **or**: *north – south, pony – horse, orange – banana, shorts – shirt, door – house, more – less,* etc. List the child's responses. Have them underline **or** in each word.

Phonics Activities:

- Have the child name a word with the **or** sound to complete each of the following sentences: *The sun comes up in the _____(morning). Cowboys ride on _____(horses). We buy food in a _____(store). I eat my pie with a _____(fork).* List the child's responses. Have them underline **or** in each word.
- Pronounce the following compound words and write them on a chalkboard or dry-erase board; include picture clues. Have the child tell whether they hear **or** in the first or second part: *shortcake, popcorn, seashore, shortstop, bookstore, storybook, cornbread.* List words as the child responds. Have them underline **or** in each word.
- For two or more children. Make a game board with one-syllable **ar**, **ir**, and **or** words written in spaces leading to a finish line. Have an accompanying set of cards with one of the three sounds written on each. A player draws a card and moves a marker to the next space having an appropriate word for the sound they have drawn. In order to claim the space, the player must decode the word. The winner is the first one to reach the finish line.

Additional Resources:

- Bailey, Donna. *Track & Field.* Orlando, FL: Raintree Steck-Vaughn Publishers, 1991.
- Ettinger, Tom, and William Jaspersohn. *My Soccer Book.* New York: HarperCollins Children's Books, 1993.
- Raatma, Lucia. *Safety at the Swimming Pool.* Mankato, MN: Capstone Press, Inc., 1999.

Published in 2002 by The Rosen Publishing Group, Inc.
29 East 21st Street, New York, NY 10010

Book Design: Ron A. Churley

Photo Credits: Cover (center and right), p. 3 (upper right) © Eyewire; Cover (left) © Rudi Von Briel/PhotoEdit/Picture Quest; p. 3 (upper left) © Ellen Skye/Index Stock; p. 3 (lower right) © Table Mesa Prod./Index Stock; p. 3 (lower left) © Bob Jacobson/Index Stock; pp. 5, 21 (right) © Marc Romanelli/Image Bank; p. 7 © D2 Productions/Index Stock; p. 9 © Gary D. Ercole/Index Stock; p. 11 © BK Productions/International Stock; p. 13 © Aneal Vohra/Index Stock; p. 15 © Omni Photo Communications, Inc./Index Stock; p. 17 © Tracy Frankel; p. 19 © Liysa King/Image Bank; p. 21 (left) © Victor Ramos/International Stock.

Library of Congress Cataloging-in-Publication Data

Hogenkamp, Susan.
    All sorts of sports : learning the OR sound / Susan Hogenkamp.
        p. cm. — (Power phonics/phonics for the real world)
    ISBN 0-8239-5949-X
    ISBN 0-8239-8294-7 (pbk.)
    6-pack ISBN 0-8239-9262-4
    1. Sports—Juvenile literature. [1. Sports.]
    I. Title. II. Series.
    GV705.4.H63 2001   2001-916
    796—dc21

Manufactured in the United States of America